Lucido
greeting cards

Jannie van Schuylenburg-Dekker

FORTE PUBLISHERS

Contents

© 2004 Forte Uitgevers, Utrecht
© 2004 for the translation by the publisher
Original title: *Lucido wenskaarten*

All rights reserved. No part of this publication may be copied, stored in an electronic file or made public, in any form or in any way whatsoever, either electronically, mechanically, by photocopying or any other form of recording, without the publisher's prior written permission.

Second printing January 2005
ISBN 90 5877 453 8

This is a publication from
Forte Publishers BV
P.O. Box 1394
3500 BJ Utrecht
The Netherlands

For more information about the creative books available from Forte Uitgevers:
www.forteuitgevers.nl

Final editing: Gina Kors-Lambers, Steenwijk, the Netherlands
Photography and digital image editing: Fotografie Gerhard Witteveen, Apeldoorn, the Netherlands
Cover and inner design:
BADE creatieve communicatie, Baarn, the Netherlands
Translation: Michael Ford, TextCase, Hilversum, the Netherlands

Preface	3
Techniques	4
Step-by-step	5
Materials	7
Cards on the cover	7
Warm pink	8
Scrapbooking with Lucido	11
Clear blue	15
Lucido with different paper	18
As green as grass	22
Sunny yellow	24
Christmas in red	27
Christmas in green	30

Preface

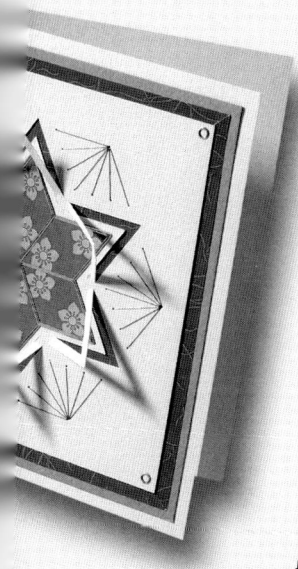

Sometimes, a word or a comment is enough for the creation of a new idea. That is exactly what happened with Lucido. A simple comment about pieces of paper grew into something much bigger. I could see the result myself: a sort of stained glass. But where do you go from there? After some discussion, it was decided to design some templates to give the idea more structure. Stickers and paper were also needed. Once I got started with my own materials, even more ideas came bubbling to the surface. That's how it should be with all the crafting material. You should also try to use them in a different way, because that leads to new ideas. I hope that you are as enthusiastic about Lucido as I am. Lucido: simplicity with an attractive result.

Have fun.

Jannie

Many thanks to: My family, who endured much, but also helped and gave useful comments; Marieke and Guda for being there when I needed you; My students for their trust and ideas; Marianne Perlot, who sent my first cards to Kars which got the ball rolling; Harald for pushing me and supporting me and the many others who have helped me along the way.

Techniques

Lucido (Spanish for crystal clear) is a technique for producing a stained glass impression using pieces of paper and line stickers.
The cards are made in the following order:
1. Copy the pattern and the centre lines onto the card and then prick the embroidery holes.
2. Embossing, 3. Embroidering, 4. Draw the segments, cut them out and stick them on the card.
5. Decorate the pattern with a Lucido sticker.

Copying the patterns

Cut card to the correct size (use thin card when embossing). Use template tape to stick the card to the template. Copy a pattern (of your choice) from the middle of the template onto the card. Use a propelling pencil, because this has a thin point. There are horizontal and vertical lines on the template. Copy these onto the card and join them together to produce the centre lines. These are necessary in order to stick the pieces of paper exactly in the middle. Prick the holes. The embroidery is done later.

Embossing

Emboss a number of corners, borders or, if possible, the edge of the large pattern. To do so, place the template on a light box and use template tape to stick the card to the template. Rub the embossing stylus first over a candle to make the embossing easier (repeat this as often as necessary). Push the large stylus around the edges and the middle of the pattern. Go around the edges again using the small stylus to make the embossing sharper. Finally, remove the template from the light box and the card. You do not need a light box when embossing vellum.

Embroidery

Embroider the pattern as indicated on the template using metallic thread. Stick the thread to the back of the card using adhesive tape. To prevent the thread from coming loose, fold the thread back over the tape and stick it down again. Do this again once you have finished. Finally, push the holes closed from the back of the card.

Segments

The large shape is made from a number of segments. These segments are punched into the edge of the template in different sizes. Templates 02 and 04 have segments with a letter. Look at the pictures to see which letters you need. This is also written on the back of the template packaging. In this book, the required segments are stated with every description, but pay attention to this if you want to experiment

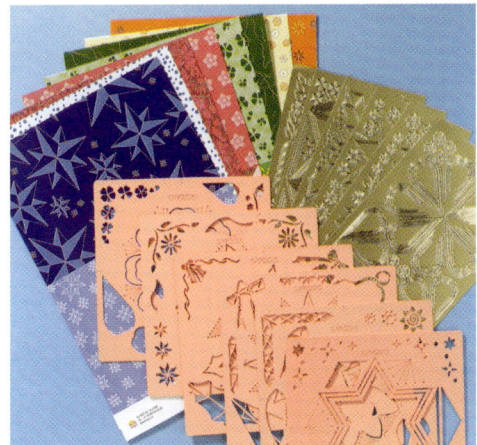

1. The new Lucido materials.

2. Use a propelling pencil to draw the template pattern, the centre lines and the segments.

3. Cut out the segments and stick them on the card.

4. Use Lucido stickers to decorate the flower: first the open pieces and then the closed pieces.

yourself. Use a propelling pencil to draw the matching segments as often as necessary or as often as indicated on the front of the Lucido paper. Keep the good side of the template facing upwards, because otherwise, for some templates, the stickers will no longer fit. Cut the segments out carefully and stick them on the card in the pattern you have drawn. I find it easier to stick them down alternately: first one colour and then the other colour in between. Make sure the segments touch the centre lines.

Lucido stickers

Decorate the edges of the segments with the matching stickers. Look to see which segment stickers you need. They are almost always put together in a rosette shape. Use a knife to remove the segment stickers from the sheet and carefully stick them on the edges of the segments. The stickers can be shaped a little bit. Where necessary, start with the open/separate segments. When there are a number of open segments, start from the outside. The other segment stickers will then be stuck over the ends. Finally, use the closed parts. These are used to cover the ends of the separate pieces. Decorate the card with line stickers, sticker dots, flowers or stars. Also use a knife to do this.

Scoring

Scoring is making a groove in the card using a ruler and a small embossing stylus or the point of a pair of scissors. The card can then be easily folded without making any creases. This is certainly recommended when a card is to be folded.

Matting

The term matting is used for scrapbooking. This means that a larger piece of card is stuck under the photograph and is then cut to create a wide or narrow border. You can make as many layers as you wish. In the Scrapbooking with Lucido chapter, you can choose the colour and the size which best suits your photographs.

Gluing tip

Do the following to apply glue to a small bit of loose paper without making a mess.
Add a small drop of glue to the edge of a small piece of scrap card. Slide the scrap piece of card under the loose bit of paper and then remove it again. There will then be enough glue under the paper to stick it down but not so much that it will come out from under the edges. You can also do this for the separate middle pieces.

Materials

- Card: cArt-us (C) and Papicolor (P)
- Vellum
- Lucido templates 01 to 06
- Lucido stickers 01 to 06 and Lucido paper 01 to 08
- Straight decorative line stickers
- Various types of paper
- Various types of scrapbook paper
- Sulky metallic thread
- Organza ribbon
- Twistart twisted paper
- Double-sided adhesive tape
- Foam tape
- Template tape
- Hobby glue
- Photo glue
- Gold gel pen
- Eyelets
- Eyelet toolkit
- Corner punches
- Punch/revolving hole punch
- Light box
- Embossing stylus
- Prick mat and prick pen
- Cutting mat
- Olfa design knife
- Ruler
- Tweezers
- Scissors
- Propelling pencil
- Rubber
- Candle

Cards on the cover

Square card with a frame
Template: LU 02 • Sticker: LU ST 02 • Paper: LUPA 07 and 08 • Card: dark red C0519 (14 x 14 cm double card), warm pink C0485 (13.5 x 13.5 cm) and pink C0481 (13.5 x 13.5 cm) • Sulky thread: Christmas red 7014 • Gold gel pen

Cut a square (9 x 9 cm) out of the front of the double card. Stick the warm pink card behind the opening and cut a square out of it to create a 2 mm border. Draw the largest flower on the pink card. Prick and embroider the pattern. Draw segments c and d five times on paper of two different colours. Cut them out and stick them on the pink flower. Decorate the flower with the stickers. Stick the pink card inside the double card. Use the gel pen and sticker dots to decorate the card.

Card with four windows
Template: LU 02 • Sticker: LU ST 02 • Paper: LUPA 07 and 08 • Card: dark red C0519 (14.8 x 14.8 cm double card) and natural C0211 (14.5 x 14.5 cm)
Draw a pencil line around the inside of the front of the dark red double card 1 cm from the edge. Cut out four squares (6 x 6 cm) using the pencil line as the edge. Place the natural card in the dark red card and copy the squares. Use the template to draw the smallest flower in three squares. Draw segments a and b five times on paper and cut them out. Draw segments g and e five times on paper of two different colours. Cut them out and stick them on the flowers. Use the matching stickers to decorate the flowers. Emboss four large and four small suns in the fourth square. Rub out all the pencil lines and stick the natural card in the dark red card.

Warm pink

From very light to very dark.

1. Zigzag card with a pink sun
Template: LU 03 • Sticker: LU ST 03 • Paper: LUPA 07 and 08 • Card: warm pink C0485 (10.5 x 14.8 cm double card), pink C0481 (10.5 x 14.8 cm) and white C0210 (9 x 9 cm)
Draw the middle flower on white card and emboss the edge of the outer flower. Cut the flower out leaving a 1 mm border. Draw the middle segment four times on card of two different colours. Cut them out and stick them on the flower. Use stickers to decorate the flower. Stick the flower in the middle of the inside of the front of the double card. Score a line from the top to the bottom of the card, but do not score the flower. Cut around the right-hand side of the flower, 1 mm from the flower, and fold the left-hand side of the score line forwards. Cut 2 mm from the edge of the pink card and stick this strip to the front of the card on the left-hand side. Stick the rest of the pink

WARM PINK

Segment diagram: template 02

a+b or c+d

e or f

g

card inside the card against the fold. Decorate the card with border stickers.

2. Gold and pink star
Template: LU 04 • Sticker: LU ST 04 • Paper: LUPA 07 • Gold paper • Card: warm pink C0485 (14 x 14 cm double card), dark red C0519 (13 x 13 cm) and pink C0481 (10.5 x 10.5 cm)
Draw the outer star on pink card (10.5 x 10.5 cm). Draw segments d and e four times on pink card and four times on gold paper. Stick the segments d on the star first and then the segments e against them in the corners. Decorate the segments with stickers. Cut triangles (3 x 3 cm) off the corners of the card. Stick the card and the cut off triangles on dark red card. Stick the dark red card on the warm pink double card and stick line stickers around the octagon.

3. Star with separate points
Template: LU 06 • Sticker: LU ST 06 • Paper: LUPA 07 and 08 • Card: pink C0481 (14.5 x 14.5 cm double card), pink C0481 (12 x 12 cm) and warm pink C0485 (13.5 x 13.5 cm)
• Sulky thread: Christmas red 7014
Draw the smallest star on pink card (12 x 12 cm) and use the template to cut the lines of the two largest stars. Prick and embroider the pattern. Draw the smallest segment six times and stick them on the star. Cut four 1 cm wide strips and a square (10 x 10 cm) from the Lucido paper. Stick the square behind the star. Draw a pencil line around the back of the card 0.5 cm from the edge. Stick the strips along the line, so that 0.5 cm protrudes from the back. Do not stick the corners down yet. Slide a piece of card between the paper and the card and then carefully cut both corners at an angle. Fold the points of the star forwards. Stick everything on the card and decorate the card with the stickers.

4. Dark red flower on white
Template: LU 01 • Sticker: LU ST 01 • Paper: LUPA 07 and 08 • Card: dark red C0519 (14.8 x 14.8 cm double card), warm pink C0485

(13.7 x 13.7 cm) and white C0210 (13 x 13 cm)
• Sulky thread: Gold 7007
Place the template on the white card and draw the largest shape. Prick and embroider the pattern. Emboss the branch on the left and right-hand sides. Draw the largest segment four times on card of two different colours. Stick them on the flower and decorate the flower with the stickers. Stick all the pieces together and stick sticker dots in the corners.

5. Vellum card with a ribbon
Template: LU 02 • Sticker LU ST 02 • Paper: LUPA 08 • Card: soft pink C0480 (13 x 13 cm double card) • Vellum: rock candy pink P150 (13 x 13 cm double card) • White Organza ribbon: 2.5 cm wide and 50 cm long
Place the template on the front of the vellum card and cut out the largest flower. Emboss the holes and emboss the edge of the flower four times. Place the template on the front of the soft pink card and draw the smallest flower. Draw segment g eight times. Cut them out and stick them on the flower. Use the stickers to decorate the flower. Slide the cards together and use a hole punch to punch two holes 6 cm apart. Thread the Organza ribbon through the holes and tie it into a bow.

Scrapbooking with Lucido

Choose a colour and size of paper which best suits your photographs.

1. Lilies
Template: LU 03 • Sticker: LU ST 03 • Paper: LUPA 07 and 08 • Card: wine red P36 (13 x 15 cm for matting and three squares 6 x 6 cm) and pink C0481 (9 x 17 cm, 8 x 8 cm and 13 x 15 cm for matting and three squares 5.5 x 5.5 cm)

• Sharon Ann scrapbook paper: crimson paper linen border and crimson paper linen • Vellum: natural (for the text) • White Twistart • Quickutz tool and letter set (Phoebe) • Photo glue

Draw the smallest flower on the pink cards. Draw the smallest segment four times for each flower on Lucido paper of two different colours and cut them out. Stick the segments on the flowers and decorate them with the stickers. Stick the flowers on the wine red cards. Make a mat for the large photograph using the pink and the wine red cards. Make a mat for the small photograph using the pink card and stick it on the pink strip. Print the text on the vellum, tear it out and stick it above the photograph on the pink strip. Tear a strip (3 x 9 cm) out of the crimson linen and stick this above the vellum. Make the letters and stick them on the crimson linen. Take 35 cm of Twistart and untwist it slightly. Draw a vertical line on the scrapbook paper 1.5 cm from the edge and stick the Twistart on the line. Also stick a piece of Twistart next to the text. Stick all the pieces on the scrapbook paper.

2. Splashing water

Template: LU 02 • Sticker: LU ST 02 • Paper: LUPA 07 • Card: silver grey P02 (11 x 15.5 cm and 7 x 7 cm) and dark red C0519 (15 x 19.5 cm and 6 x 6 cm) • Sharon Ann scrapbook paper: soft sage page woven lint, soft sage paper linen: four 2 cm wide strips, a piece of 8.5 x 16.5 cm and a circle (Ø 3 cm) • Vellum: natural (10 x 20 cm) for the text • Lime green Twistart • Quickutz tool and letter set (Phoebe) • Photo glue • Eyelets • Gold cord

Draw the smallest flower on dark red card (6 x 6 cm). Draw segment a five times on a photograph and segment b five times on Lucido paper and cut them out. Stick them on the flower and decorate the flower with some stickers. Cut the flower out along the edge of the stickers. Use silver grey and dark red card to make mats for the photograph. Draw a pencil line around the back of the dark red card 1 cm from the edge. Stick the strips of sage linen paper on the pencil line, but do not stick it down in the corners (everything will protrude by 1 cm). Place a scrap piece of card in the corner between the strips of paper and the card. Cut both strips at an angle and remove the scrap piece of card. Do this for all the corners. Write the text on the vellum and tear it so that it measures 7.5 x 15.5 cm. Stick it on the piece of sage linen paper (8.5 x 16.5 cm). Stick the photographs and the piece of text on the scrapbook paper. Untwist the Twistart. Stick the green circle on a piece of card and cut it out. Make four holes in the middle and decorate it with circle stickers or eyelets. Thread the Twistart through it. Stick the thread and the button on the card as shown in the photograph. Use the flower to make a label by sticking gold cord behind it and then stick it on the silver grey card. Cut the silver grey card out leaving a border and stick the label in place. Use an eyelet to keep the cord in place. Use the Quickutz tool to make the letters and stick them on the card.

Clear blue

It is still one of my favourite colours.

1. Star with a light centre
Template: LU 04 • Sticker: LU ST 04 • Paper: LUPA 01 and 02 • Card: aqua blue C0427 (14 x 14 cm double card and 10 x 10 cm) and white C0210 (10 x 10 cm) • Sulky thread: gold 7007 • Foam tape
Draw the inner star on aqua blue paper and cut it out along the lines of the outer star. Draw segment a eight times on light-coloured paper and segments b and c four times on dark-coloured paper and cut them out. Stick segments a in the middle and segments b and c around them. Decorate the segments with stickers. Prick and embroider the patterns on the white card (10 x 10 cm) and emboss the corners. Stick this on the double card. Stick the star on the card using foam tape. Decorate the card with line stickers.

2. Blue sun
Template: LU 03 • Sticker: LU ST 03 • Paper: LUPA 01 and 02 • Card: aqua blue C0427 (14 x 14 cm double card) and white C0210 (13 x 13 cm) • Sulky thread: blue 7016
Draw the middle flower on the white card. Emboss the edge of the outer flower and the four corners. Prick and embroider the patterns. Draw the middle segment four times on card of two different colours. Cut them out and stick them on the flower. Stick the white card on the double card and decorate the card with stickers and dots.

3. Double flower
Template: LU 01 • Stickers: LU ST 01 • Paper: LUPA 02 • Card: lavender P21 (10.5 x 14.8 cm double card), white C0210 (8 x 8 cm and 6 x 6 cm) and aqua blue C0427 (8 x 12.5 cm) • Sulky thread: gold 7007 • Foam tape
Draw the middle and the smallest flowers on the white cards. Draw the middle and the smallest segments eight times on Lucido paper and cut them out. Stick them on the white flowers and decorate them with stickers. Cut the smallest flower out and use foam tape to stick it at an angle on the middle flower. Prick and embroider the four corners of the aqua blue card and stick it on the double card. Decorate the small card with sticker dots and use foam tape to stick it on the card with a corner facing upwards.

4. Tumbling blocks
Template: LU 06 • Sticker: LU ST 06 • Paper: LUPA 01 and 02 • Card: aqua blue C0427 (14 x 14 cm double card and 6 x 6 cm) and white

Segment diagram: template 04

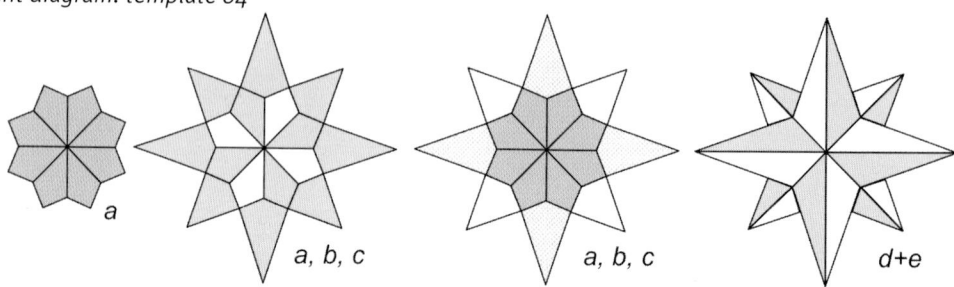

C0210 (12 x 12 cm and 6 x 6 cm) • Gold cord
• Double fly corner punch
Draw the middle star on white card (12 x 12 cm). Draw the middle segment four times on three different types of paper and cut them out. Fill the star with two segments of the same colour opposite each other. Stick three different segments in the three corners to create cubes. Stick the last three segments in the shape of a cube on the small white card and cut it out leaving a 0.5 cm border. Stick this on the blue card with a gold cord in between and cut it out leaving a 3 mm border. Decorate everything with stickers. Cut a diamond shape in two lengthways. Punch the corners of the white card and stick it on the double card. Attach the label to the left-hand corner of the card.

5. Blue with two flowers
Template: LU 02 • Sticker: LU ST 02 • Paper: LUPA 01 and 02 • Card: aqua blue C0427 (10.5 x 14.8 cm double card), dark blue C0417 (10 x 14.8 cm) and white C0210 (6 x 6 cm twice) • Gold gel pen
Draw the smallest flower on both white cards. Draw segments g and e five times on paper of two different colours and cut them out. Stick them on the flowers and decorate them with the stickers. Cut the flowers out by placing the ruler 2 mm from the points of the petals to create a decagon. Cut four small flower stickers into five and use them to decorate the flower circles. Draw a slanting line from the top left-hand corner to the bottom right-hand corner of the front of the card and stick the flowers on it. Cut along the line leaving a 1 mm border around the flowers. Stick the dark blue card inside the card to create a 2 mm border on the right-hand side. Decorate the corners of the card with leaf stickers and use a gel pen to draw around the flowers.

CLEAR BLUE 17

Lucido with different paper

You can use anything.

1. Flower with embroidered paper
*Template: LU 02 • Sticker: LU ST 02
• Embroidered paper • Card: ochre C0575 (14 x 14 cm double card) and natural C0211 (13 x 13 cm) • Sulky thread: light copper 7011*
Draw the largest flower on natural card. Prick the embroidery pattern on every other petal. Rotate the template by one petal and prick the same pattern again so that all the patterns face the same direction. Embroider the patterns. Emboss the flower border around the edge of the card. Draw segments c and d five times on embroidered paper and cut them out. Stick them on the flower and decorate them with stickers. Stick the cards together and add some sticker dots.

2. Card with a label
Template: LU 03 • Sticker: LU ST 03 • Déjà Views FP 2000 • Provo Craft scrap pad 40-1078 • Card: dark blue C0417 (10.5 x 14.8 cm double card, 6 x 9 cm and scrap pieces for the suns), and ochre C0575 (9 x 13.5 cm) • Gold cord • Gold eyelets • Foam tape
Stick the ochre card on the dark blue double card. Make a hole and punch an eyelet in the dark blue card (6 x 9 cm). Thread a cord through the eyelet and decorate the card with line stickers. Stick the label on the card. Draw the smallest and the middle flowers on the scrap pieces of card. Draw the smallest segment eight times on flower paper and the middle segment eight times on blue paper. Stick them on the flowers and decorate them with stickers. Cut them out and use foam tape to stick them on the card.

3. Blue card with a flower
Template: LU 02 • Sticker: LU ST 02 • Déjà Views paper FP 2000 • Provo Craft scrap pad 40-1078 • Card: dark blue C0417 (10.5 x 14.8 cm double card and 8 x 12.5 cm) • Provo Craft paper (9.5 x 14 cm)

Stick the Provo Craft paper and the blue card on the double card. Draw the smallest flower on the blue card. Draw segments a and b five times on paper of two different colours and cut them out. Stick them on the flower and decorate the flower with the stickers and the card with sticker dots.

4. Red sun with vellum
Template: LU 03 • Sticker: LU ST 03 • Red and dark red fibre paper • Card: Christmas red P43 (14 x 14 cm double card) and ochre C0575 (13 x 13 cm and 12 x 12 cm) • Natural vellum (13.5 x 13.5 cm)

Make a 2 cm wide frame from the ochre card (13 x 13 cm). Stick this frame on the Christmas red card and cut out the middle leaving a 2 mm border. Draw the middle sun exactly in the middle of the vellum and emboss the lines of the largest sun. Draw the middle segment four times on red and dark red fibre paper and cut them out. Stick them on the vellum and decorate them with stickers. Stick the vellum inside the front of the card against the opening and the small ochre card against the back of the card. Decorate the card with some stickers.

5. White frame card with a red flower
Template: LU 01 • Sticker: LU ST 01 • Paper: han-ji paper • Card: natural C0211 (14 x 14 cm double card) and Christmas red P43 (13.8 x 13.8 cm and 10 x 10 cm) • Foam tape

Make a 2.3 cm frame in the front of the double card. Stick the cut out square inside the card. Emboss the flower border around the frame. Stick the Christmas red card behind the frame and cut out the middle leaving a 2 mm border. Draw the largest flower on the Christmas red card. Draw the largest segment eight times on han-ji paper and stick them on the flower. Decorate the flower with the stickers and cut it out along the stickers. Use foam tape to stick it on the card.

20 LUCIDO WITH DIFFERENT PAPER

AS GREEN AS GRASS

As green as grass

It comes in all colours.

1. Card with squares and a sliding square
Template: LU 06 • Sticker: LU ST 06 • Paper: LUPA 03 and 04 • Gold paper • Card: green C0367 (10.5 x 14.8 cm double card), natural C0211 (5.5 x 13.5 cm and scrap pieces) and gold gloss card C9104 (6 x 14 cm) • 30 cm of 3 mm wide gold ribbon • Narrow double-sided adhesive tape

Draw the smallest segment four times on card of three different colours and cut them out. Stick nine segments on the natural strip (5.5 x 13.5 cm) to make three cubes. Stick the last three segments on the scrap piece of natural card to make a cube. Decorate the cubes with stickers. Cut out the separate cube. Stick the gold card and the natural strip together and then stick them on the green double card. Mark the width of the ribbon on the back of the separate cube and stick double-sided adhesive tape to the left and right of the mark. Place the ribbon between the tape and then stick a scrap piece of card on top. The cube will now be able to slide along the ribbon. Use double-sided adhesive tape to stick the top and bottom 2 cm of the ribbon on the left-hand side of the card so that the cube will remain between these points. Fold the rest of the ribbon behind the card and stick it down using double-sided adhesive tape.

2. Flower card with an opening
Template: LU 01 • Sticker: LU ST 01 • Paper: LUPA 04 • Card: dark green C0309 (14 x 14 cm double card), old red C0517 (13.5 x 13.5 cm, 7 x 7 cm and 3.5 x 7 cm) and natural C0211 (13.5 x 13.5 cm, 6.5 x 6.5 cm and 3 x 6.5 cm) • Sulky thread: Christmas green 7018

Cut a rectangle (3 x 12 cm) out of the front of the dark green card 1.5 cm from the right-hand side. Stick the old red card (13.5 x 13.5 cm) behind the opening and cut it to leave a 2 mm wide border. Place the natural card (13.5 x 13.5 cm) in the double card and mark the opening. Emboss the branch in the frame and stick the card in the double card. Draw the smallest flower on the natural square (6.5 x 6.5 cm). Draw the smallest segment four times on card of two different colours. Cut them out and stick them on the flower. Use stickers to decorate the flower. Embroider three patterns, 2 cm apart, on the smallest natural strip. Stick the natural cards on the old red cards and stick them on the green card. Decorate everything with sticker dots.

3. Green sun
Template: LU 03 • Sticker: LU ST 03 • Paper: LUPA 03 and 04 • Card: green C0367 (14 x 14 cm double card) and white C0210 (12 x 12 cm) • Sulky thread: gold 7007

Use the template to draw the largest flower on white card. Emboss the corners. Prick and embroider the patterns in the card. Draw the largest segment four times on card of two different colours and cut them out. Stick them on the white card and decorate the flower with stickers. Stick the white card on the green double card. Stick a border sticker around it and stick sticker dots in the corners.

4. Card with raffia
Template: LU 05 • Sticker: LU ST 05 • Paper: LUPA 03 • Card: snow white P30 (10.5 x 18.5 cm and 7.5 x 7.5 cm), grass green P07 (10.5 x 14.8 cm and 5 x 5 cm) and Structura fern green P137 (4.5 x 4.5 cm) • Sulky thread: Christmas green 7018 • Raffia • Narrow double-sided adhesive tape

Score the short side of the snow white card 3.5 cm from the edge and fold it over. Use double-sided adhesive tape to stick grass green card (10.5 x 14.8 cm) against the fold of the card. Make two holes, 6 cm apart, in the front of the card near the fold and thread the raffia through them. Emboss the corners of the snow white square card. Prick and embroider the pattern in the fern green card (4.5 x 4.5 cm). Stick sticker dots in the corners. Stick the fern green card on the grass green card and then on the snow white card. Stick everything on the card. Draw the smallest holly leaf three times and cut them out. Stick them on the white border and decorate them with stickers.

5. Yellow and green star
Template: LU 04 • Sticker: LU ST 04 • Paper: LUPA 03 and 05 • Card: snow white P30 (14 x 14 cm double card and 12.5 x 12.5 cm) and Structura fern green (13.5 x 13.5 cm) • Sulky thread: Christmas red 7018

Place the template on the snow white card (12.5 x 12.5 cm) and draw the largest star. Emboss the pattern in the middle of the four sides. Prick and embroider the pattern around the star and in the corners. Draw segments d and e four times on yellow card and four times on green paper. Stick segments d on the star first and then stick segments e against them in the corners. Decorate the star with the stickers. Draw a diagonal line in the corners, 4 cm from the points, and cut along the lines. Stick the triangles and the star on the fern green card and stick this on the snow white double card. Decorate the card with line stickers.

Sunny yellow

This colour will cheer you up!

1. Yellow flower with loose petals
Template: LU 02 • Sticker: LU ST 02 • Paper: LUPA 05 and 06 • Card: yellow C0275 (14.5 x 14.5 cm double card), ochre C0575 (13.6 x 13.6 cm) and white C0210 (13 x 13 cm) • Sulky thread: pale copper 7011

Place the template on the white card and draw the smallest flower. Use the template to cut the petals of the largest flower. Prick and embroider the patterns, making sure the thread does not go under the incision of the large petals. Emboss three suns in the corners. Draw segments a and b five times on Lucido paper and cut them out. Stick them on the flower and decorate the flower with stickers and the outer petals with sticker dots. Bend the petals slightly forwards. Stick everything together.

2. Double orange and yellow sun
Template: LU 03 • Sticker: LU ST 03 • Paper: LUPA 05 and 06 • Card: yellow C0275 (10.5 x 14.8 cm double card, two pieces of 7.5 x 7.5 cm and 5 x 5 cm), orange C0545 (7.8 x 7.8 cm) and dark red C0519 (5 x 14.8 cm) • Foam tape

Draw the smallest flower on the yellow card (5 x 5 cm) and the middle flower on the yellow card (7.5 x 7.5 cm.) Draw the smallest segment eight times on orange paper and the middle segment eight times on yellow paper. Cut them out and stick them on the corresponding flower. Use stickers to decorate the flowers. Cut out the smallest flower and use foam tape to stick it on the yellow flower. Stick the yellow card on the orange card and stick sticker dots in the corners. Stick the dark red strip in the middle of the double yellow card. Decorate the strip with line stickers. Use foam tape to stick the square card at an angle on the double card.

3. Flower in a folded corner
Templates: LU 01 and 03 • Stickers: LU ST 01 and 03 • Paper: LUPA 05 • Card: golden yellow C0247 (14 x 14 cm double card and 6 x 6 cm) and fiesta red P12 (13.5 x 13.5 and 6 x 6 cm) • Foam tape

Draw two lines on the front of the card, one which is 1.5 cm from the edge and one which is 3 cm form the edge. Draw a diagonal line 13 cm from the top right-hand corner to the top left-hand corner. Score the top and bottom of the diagonal line making sure not to go over the line which was drawn 3 cm from the edge. Cut the pencil line which is 3 cm from the edge and fold the corner over and back again.

SUNNY YELLOW 25

Use template 03 to emboss the middle segment on the line which was drawn 1.5 cm from the edge. Emboss another small flower in the embossed segments. Rub out the lines. Fold the corner over. Stick the fiesta red card (13.5 x 13.5 cm) in the golden yellow card and draw a line at the top and on the right-hand side 1.2 cm from the edge. Draw the middle segment of template 03 six times on paper and cut them out. Stick them on the pencil line on the red card. Use stickers to decorate the segments. Stick the small red card in the middle of the double card. Use template 01 to draw the smallest flower on the small yellow card. Draw the smallest segment eight times on paper of two different colours and cut them out. Stick them on the small card and decorate the flower with stickers. Cut out the flower and use foam tape to stick it in the middle of the red card.

4. Large orange and yellow flower

Template: LU 02 • Sticker: LU ST 02 • Paper: LUPA 05 and 06 • Card: golden yellow C0247 (10.5 x 14.8 cm double card), terracotta C0549 (9.8 x 14.3 cm) and carnation white P03 (9.5 x 13.9 cm)

Draw the largest flower on the carnation white card. Emboss the suns in the top corners and a flower border along the bottom edge. Draw segments c and d five times on orange and yellow paper and cut them out. Stick them on the card and decorate the flower with the stickers. Stick everything together and stick stickers on the flower border.

5. Yellow and green sun

Template: U 03 • Sticker: LU ST 03 • Paper: LUPA 03 and 06 • Card: golden yellow C0247 (14.5 x 14.5 cm double card), green C0367 (13.5 x 13.5 cm) and white C0210 (13 x 13 cm) • Sulky thread: Christmas red 7018

Place the template on the white card and draw the middle flower. Emboss the edges of the largest flower and emboss a flower and petals in the corners. Prick and embroider the pattern. Draw the middle segment four times on yellow card and four times on green card. Cut them out and stick them on the flower. Stick everything together and decorate the card and the flower with stickers and sticker dots.

Christmas in red

Traditional and attractive

1. Red star on a white card
Template: LU 06 • Sticker: LU ST 06 • Paper: LUPA 07 and 08 • Card: Christmas red P43 (14 x 14 cm double card) and snow white P29 (13 x 13 cm) • Sulky thread: gold 7007
Draw the largest star on the snow white card. Emboss stars in the corners. Prick and embroider the patterns with gold thread. Draw the largest segments six times on two different shades of red card and stick them on the star. Use stickers to decorate the star. Stick the white card on the Christmas red double card.

2. Green holly leaves
Template: LU 05 • Sticker: LU ST 05 • Paper: LUPA 05 • Card: wine red P36 (10.5 x 14.8 cm double card), natural Co211 (9.5 x 14.3 cm and 6 x 10.5 cm) and Christmas red P43 (10 x 14.5 cm) • Coluzzle rectangle ornament • Coluzzle cutting mat • Coluzzle swivel knife
Use the Coluzzle template to cut the smallest shape out of the smallest natural card. Emboss a bow in the top left-hand corner. Cut the third groove of the Coluzzle template (counting from the inside) into the Christmas red card. Cut the corners of the third groove of the Coluzzle template in the corners of the largest natural card. Stick all the cards together and then stick them on the wine red double card. Draw the smallest holly leaf three times on Lucido paper and cut them out. Stick them in the middle of the card. Decorate the holly leaves and the rest of the card with matching stickers.

3. Card with red squares and a star
Template: LU 06 • Sticker: LU ST 06 • Paper: LUPA 07 • Gold paper • Card: natural Co211 (14 x 14 cm double card and 8 x 8 cm), Christmas red P43 (nine pieces of 4 x 4 cm) and gold matt card 9207 (13 x 13 cm, 8.5 x 8.5 cm) • Foam tape
Draw the smallest star on natural card (8 x 8 cm). Draw the smallest segment three times on red paper and three times on gold paper and cut them through the middle. Stick them on the natural card and decorate them with stickers. Stick line stickers around the edge. Stick the card on the gold matt card (8.5 x 8.5 cm). Stick the gold matt card (13 x 13 cm) on the double card and stick the nine pieces of Christmas red card on it. Use foam tape to stick the star in the top left-hand corner of the double card.

4. Red star with a gold heart
Template: LU 04 • Sticker LU ST 04 • Paper: LUPA 07 • Gold paper • Card: dark red C0519 (10.5 x 14.8 cm double card, 10 x 10 cm and 3 x 5.5 cm) and natural C0211 (9.7 x 14 cm and 2.5 x 5 cm) • Sulky thread: gold 7007 • Double bow corner punch • Foam tape

Draw both stars on dark red card (10 x 10 cm) and cut out the largest star. Draw segment a eight times on gold card and segments b and c four times on red paper. Cut them out. Stick segments a in the middle and segments b and c around them. Use stickers to decorate the star. Prick and embroider the patterns on the natural card (9.7 x 14 cm). Punch the top corners. Stick the natural card on the dark red double card and use foam tape to stick the star on top. Stick the small natural card on the small dark red card. Stick a text sticker on it and use foam tape to stick it on the double card.

5. Gold card with a red bow
Templates: LU 04 and 06 • Stickers: LU ST 04 and 06 • Paper: LUPA 07 • Gold paper • Card: gold matt C9207 (14 x 14 cm double card), gold gloss C9104 (6.5 x 6.5 cm) and natural C0211 (11 x 11 cm and 5.5 x 5.5 cm) • Foam tape • 50 cm of 0.5 cm wide burgundy Organza ribbon

Use template 04 to draw the smallest (inner) star on the smallest natural card. Draw segment a four times on red paper and gold card and cut them out. Stick them on the star and decorate them with the stickers. Stick the card on the gold gloss card. Use foam tape to stick this on the natural card (11 x 11 cm). Stick line and star stickers around the large natural card and stick it against the fold of the gold matt double card. Draw the smallest segment of template 06 four times on gold card and cut them out. Stick the gold segments on the right-hand side of the double card and decorate them with matching stickers. Tie the Organza ribbon around the card.

CHRISTMAS IN RED 29

Christmas in green

With gold, it is always chic.

1. Holly on white
Template: LU 05 • Sticker: LU ST 05 • Paper: LUPA 03 and 04 • Card: gold gloss C9104 (13.5 x 13.5 cm double card), dark green C0309 (12.5 x 12.5 cm) and white C0210 (12 x 12 cm) • Sulky thread: gold 7007

Draw the largest holly leaf on white card and prick and embroider the shapes. Emboss the bell in the corners. Draw the largest segment three times on card of two different colours. Cut them out and stick them alternately on the leaves. You will have enough segments to make another card. Use stickers to decorate the holly. Stick everything together and add some sticker dots.

2. Green star with raffia
Templates: LU 04 and 05 • Sticker: LU ST 04 • Paper LUPA 03 and 04 • Card: natural C0211 (10.5 x 14.8 cm double card, 4 x 4 cm and 2.5 x 3.5 cm), dark green C0309 (8 x 14.8 cm), gold matt card C9207 (14.8 x 17.5 cm) and gold gloss card C9107 (3 x 8 cm and 4.5 x 4.5 cm) • Raffia • Gold eyelets

Emboss the smallest holly leaf segments three times on the left-hand side of the natural double card. Stick the dark green card on the front of the natural card, leaving a small border by the fold. Score the gold matt card 7 cm from the edge and fold it over to make a double card (10.5 x 14.8 cm) with a narrow front. Slide both cards together. Punch two eyelets 6 cm apart to attach the front of the cards together. Thread raffia through the eyelets and tie it into a bow. Use template LU 04 to draw the smallest star on the natural square (4 x 4 cm). Draw segment a four times on light green paper and dark green card and cut them out. Stick them on the star and decorate them with the stickers. Stick the natural card on the gold gloss card and then on the front of the card. Fold the piece of gold gloss card (3 x 8 cm) double to create a booklet and stick the natural card (2.5 x 3.5 cm) on the front. Stick the text sticker on it and stick it on the card. Stick lines stickers along the edge of the green and natural cards.

3. Gold holly leaves
Template: LU 05 • Sticker: LU ST 05 • Paper: LUPA 03 • Gold paper • Card: gold matt C09207 (14 x 14 cm double card), gold gloss C9104 (7.5 x 7.5 cm) and natural C0211 (11.5 x 11.5 cm and 7 x 7 cm) • Sulky thread: gold 7007 • 2.5 cm wide gold Organza ribbon • Gold eyelets • Foam tape • Narrow double-sided adhesive tape

Prick and embroider the pattern once in the

middle of the smallest natural card. Stick it on the gold gloss card and use foam tape to stick it on the natural card. Use a piece of double-sided adhesive tape to stick the card in the bottom left-hand corner against the fold. Draw the smallest holly leaf six times on gold paper and cut them out. Stick them on the edge of the card and decorate them with stickers. Stick stars in the corners. Make two holes 6 cm apart in the front of the card. Punch eyelets in the holes and thread Organza ribbon through them. Tie it into a bow.

4. Card with four windows
Template: LU 05 • Sticker: LU ST 05 • Paper: LUPA 04 • Gold paper • Card: dark green C0309 (14 x 14 cm double card, 12 x 12 cm and 2 x 4 cm), gold gloss card C9104 (13 x 13 cm) and natural C0211 (four times 5.5 x 5.5 cm and 1.5 x 3.5 cm) • Sulky thread: Christmas gold 7007 • Foam tape
Prick and embroider the pattern once on a natural square. Emboss the bell and the bow on every natural square. Draw the smallest holly leaf twice on the last card. Draw the segments of the smallest holly leaf once on green card and gold paper and cut them out. Stick them alternately on the holly leaf and decorate them with stickers. Stick all the cards together and divide the four natural cards over the large green surface. Stick a border sticker on the gold card. Stick the two smallest cards together and use foam tape to stick them to the ribbon and write a message on the card.

5. Card with embroidered diamonds
Template: LU 06 • Sticker: LU ST 06 • Paper: LUPA 04 • Gold paper • Card: natural C0211 (14 x 14 cm double card and a scrap piece), dark green C0309 (10.5 x 10.5 cm and 8 x 9 cm) and gold matt C9207 (10 x 10 cm double card) • Sulky thread: gold 7007 • Foam tape
Draw the middle segment four times on the scrap piece of natural card. Prick and embroider the pattern in the middle of every segment. Decorate the diamonds with stickers and cut them out. Draw the smallest and the middle star on the dark green card (8 x 9 cm). Draw the smallest segment three times on green card and gold paper and cut them out. Stick them on the star and decorate them with stickers. Cut the star out along the outer pencil line. Use foam tape to stick it on the gold matt double card. Stick the dark green card inside the gold matt double card. Slide both double cards together and stick them together at the back. Use foam tape to stick the four embroidered diamonds on the border and decorate the card with some stars.

Many thanks to Kars & Co. for supplying the materials.

Shopkeepers can order the materials used from Kars & Co B.V. in Ochten, the Netherlands, Papicolor International B.V. in Utrecht, the Netherlands and Scrapbook mate (Quickutz) in Amsterdam, the Netherlands.

32 CHRISTMAS IN GREEN